Reduce, Reuse, Recycle

Energy

Alexandra Fix

www.heinemann.co.uk/library

Visit our website to find out more information about **Heinemann Library** books.

To order:

 Phone ++44 (0)1865 888066

 Send a fax to ++44 (0)1865 314091

 Visit the Heinemann Bookshop at www.heinemann.co.uk/library to browse our catalogue and order online.

First published in Great Britain by Heinemann Library, Halley Court, Jordan Hill, Oxford OX2 8EJ, part of Harcourt Education.
Heinemann is a registered trademark of Harcourt Education Ltd.

© Harcourt Education Ltd 2008
The moral right of the proprietor has been asserted.

Editorial: Cassie Mayer and Diyan Leake
Design: Steven Mead and Debbie Oatley
Picture research: Ruth Blair
Production: Duncan Gilbert

Origination: Chroma Graphics (Overseas) Pte Ltd
Printed and bound in China by South China Printing Company Ltd

ISBN 978 0 431 90753 6

12 11 10 09 08
10 9 8 7 6 5 4 3 2 1

British Library Cataloguing in Publication Data
Fix, Alexandra, 1950-
Energy. - (Reduce, reuse, recycle)
1. Energy conservation - Juvenile literature 2. Energy consumption - Juvenile literature 3. Renewable energy sources - Juvenile literature
I. Title
333.7'9137

Acknowledgements
The publishers would like to thank the following for permission to reproduce photographs: Alamy pp. **20** (Chris Fredricksson), **21** (Mark Boulton); Ardea pp. **9** (Arthur Hayward), **15** (Francois Gohier), **25** (Jack A. Bailey); Corbis pp. **4** (Ashley Cooper), **5**, **6** (Royalty Free), **7** (Royalty Free), **12** (Alberto Esteves/EPA), 18 (Steve Chenn), **22** (SIE Productions/Zefa), **23** (Tim Street-Porter/Beateworks), **24** (Paul Thompson), **26** (Royalty Free), **27** (TH-Foto/Zefa); Naturepl.com pp. **8** (Aflo), **13** (Aflo), **16** (Pete Cairns), **19** (Dave Noton); Photolibrary. com pp. **10** (Dynamic Graphics Ltd), **11** (Index Stock Imagery), **17** (Botanica), **28** (Fernando Bengoechea); Reuters p. **14** (Stefano Paltera/Handout XX).

Cover photograph reproduced with permission of Alamy/ oote boe.

The publishers would like to thank Simon Miller for his assistance in the preparation of this book.

Every effort has been made to contact copyright holders of any material reproduced in this book. Any omissions will be rectified in subsequent printings if notice is given to the publishers.

Contents

Some words are shown in bold, **like this**. You can find out what they mean by looking in the glossary.

What is energy waste?

We use energy to make things work. Nearly everything around us uses energy. Most of the energy we use comes from burning coal, oil, and natural gas.

Coal, oil, and natural gas are called **fossil fuels**.

Oil is pumped from the ground by machines such as this one.

When we use more energy than we need, we waste energy. People are using up the earth's supply of coal, oil, and natural gas. Once these sources of energy are gone, they cannot be replaced.

How do we use energy?

Natural gas is a form of energy we use to cook meals and heat or cool our homes. Oil is a form of energy we use to make big machines work, such as cars, boats, and aeroplanes.

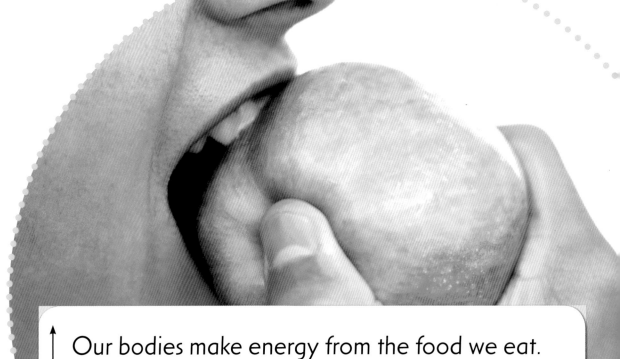

Our bodies make energy from the food we eat.

Many kitchen items need electricity to work. ↑

Electricity is a form of energy that makes many items work. Anything that plugs into the wall uses electricity. Lamps, computers, fridges, televisions, and toasters all use electricity to work.

Where does energy come from?

There are many sources of energy. These include the sun, wind, and ocean waves. We can use these sources of energy to make **electricity**.

Most of the energy on earth comes from the sun.

Dinosaur remains from long ago turned into fuel we use today.

We can also make electricity by burning coal, oil, and natural gas. These materials are called **fossil fuels**. They are the remains of animals and plants that died millions of years ago.

Nuclear power plants create energy we use to make electricity for homes, schools, and offices.

Many places use **nuclear energy** to make **electricity**. Nuclear energy comes from the energy stored inside a certain type of **atom**. Atoms are tiny, invisible particles that make up everything around us.

We can also make electricity with **geothermal energy**. This form of energy comes from hot liquid rock trapped deep inside the earth.

People can heat buildings and make electricity by pumping up heated water from deep underground.

What are non-renewable energy sources?

Most of the energy we use comes from burning coal, oil, and natural gas. These materials are **non-renewable resources**. Once we use them up they will be gone forever.

Oil is a non-renewable resource that we use to make cars work. →

People are starting to use corn as an energy source. Corn can be grown and does not pollute the air.

Non-renewable resources **pollute** the air when they are burned for energy. Scientists believe that air **pollution** is causing the earth's **climate** to change. This is called **global warming**.

What are renewable energy sources?

Some of the energy we use comes from **renewable resources**. These are resources we will never run out of. Most renewable energy sources do not cause air **pollution**.

Solar cars run on electricity made by the sun. ↓

A field of windmills can make electricity from wind power. ↑

Sunshine and wind are renewable energy sources. Both of these sources can be used to make **electricity**.

Water that makes electricity is called hydroelectric power.

Moving water is a **renewable resource**. Scientists are learning how to use ocean waves to make **electricity**. Dams and waterfalls can also be used to make electricity.

Trees and plants are renewable energy sources. We can grow more trees and plants as we use them. They can be burned to create energy.

Burning wood is the oldest use of **bioenergy**.

What happens when we waste energy?

When we waste energy, we waste **non-renewable resources** such as coal, oil, and natural gas. Once we use up these resources they will be gone forever.

We can save energy by turning down the heating in our homes.

↑ Factory smoke gives off harmful gases.

When coal, oil, and natural gas are burned they create air **pollution**. Scientists believe that this is causing **global warming**. By using less energy, we can help reduce air pollution.

How can we use less energy?

There are many ways to use less energy at home. You can use less hot water to save energy. Try washing things less often. Towels and most clothing can be used more than once.

↑ Dry clothes outside on sunny days.

Energy-saving light bulbs last longer than normal light bulbs.

Lights use energy. When you leave a room, turn off the lights. You can also ask family members to buy fluorescent light bulbs. They use less energy than normal light bulbs.

To save energy, turn off and unplug the television when you are finished watching it.

Household items may use energy even when they are not being used. Turn off **appliances** such as televisions, toasters, and stereos at the socket when you are not using them.

Use appliances that take less energy to work. Put on extra clothes instead of turning heating up. Walk or ride a bike whenever you can instead of riding in a car. Cars use oil, which is a **non-renewable resource**.

Trees near houses can help keep them cool in summer.

How can recycling save energy?

We can save energy by **recycling** products that are made out of glass, plastic, metal, and paper. It takes less energy to make items from recycled materials than it does to make new items.

Some communities have separate rubbish bins for materials that can be recycled.

When items are not recycled they are buried at a landfill site.

Separate recycling materials when you use them at home or at school. You can then take them to a recycling centre. Then they are taken to a factory where they are broken down and used to make new products.

How can you take action?

Ask family and friends to be more careful about using **electricity**. Remind others to turn off lights when they leave a room to save energy.

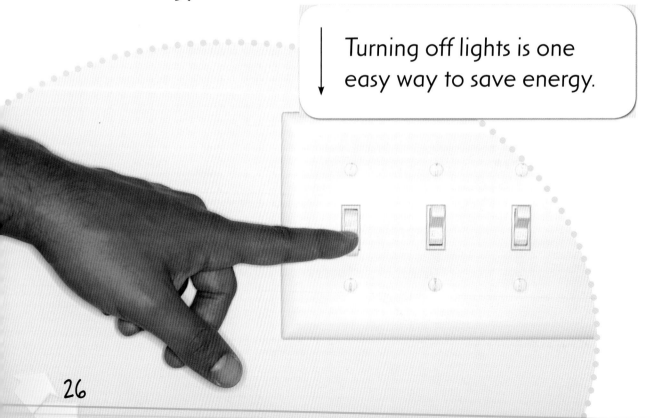

Turning off lights is one easy way to save energy.

It takes less energy to recycle plastic, glass, metal, and paper than to make them new.

Find out where your local **recycling** centre is located. You can start recycling at home and at school. By reducing energy waste, we can help to protect our planet.

Be an energy detective!

Ask an adult to help you with this project.

Complete the following steps to learn more about how much energy is used in your home.

1. Get a notebook and pencil.
2. Look around each room in your house.
3. In each room, write down everything that uses gas.

4. In each room, write down everything that uses **electricity**.

Think of ways your family can reduce the amount of energy they use. Were all the electrical items plugged in? Items that are plugged in use energy even when they are not turned on.

Fast facts

Recycling one aluminium drinks can saves enough energy to power a television for three hours.

Each UK household throws away more than one tonne of rubbish every year.

Glossary

appliance   household machine, such as a dishwasher or toaster, that usually runs on electricity or gas

atom   one of the tiny particles that makes up all things

bioenergy   living things that can be burned to create energy

climate   typical weather of a place over a period of time

electricity   form of energy that can be used to create light, heat, and power

fossil fuel   remains of animals and plants that died millions of years ago and slowly turned into coal, oil, and natural gas

geothermal energy   water heated by hot, liquid rock trapped deep inside the earth

global warming   change in the earth's climate

non-renewable resource   material taken from the earth that cannot be replaced by nature

nuclear energy   form of energy that comes from using atoms

pollute   harm the air, soil, or water with chemicals or wastes

pollution   harm the air, soil, or water with chemicals or wastes

recycling   breaking down and using again

renewable resource   material that can be replaced by nature

Find out more

Books to read

I Can Help Save Energy, Viv Smith (Franklin Watts, 2001)

Using Materials: How We Use Coal, Chris Oxlade
(Raintree, 2005)

Using Materials: How We Use Oil, Chris Oxlade
(Raintree, 2005)

Websites

Waste Watch work to teach people about reducing,
reusing, and recycling waste. You can visit
www.recyclezone.org.uk to find out more information
about waste and to try some online activities.

Find out where you can recycle in your local area at:
www.recyclenow.com by typing in your postcode. You
can also find out more about which items can be recycled,
more facts about waste, and what you can do to help!.

Index